Out of Darkness
THE STORY OF LOUIS BRAILLE

by RUSSELL FREEDMAN

Illustrated by Kate Kiesler

Clarion Books/New York

Clarion Books
a Houghton Mifflin Company imprint

Text copyright © 1997 by Russell Freedman
Illustrations copyright © 1997 by Kate Kiesler

The illustrations for this book were executed in pencil.
The text was set in 14/21-point Columbus.
All rights reserved.

Printed in the USA.

Library of Congress Cataloging-in-Publication Data
Freedman, Russell.
Out of darkness : the story of Louis Braille / by Russell Freedman ;
illustrated by Kate Kiesler.
p.   cm.
Includes index.
Summary: A biography of the nineteenth-century Frenchman who, having been blinded
himself at the age of three, went on to develop a system of raised dots on paper that
enabled blind people to read and write.
ISBN 0-395-77516-7   PA ISBN 0-395-96888-7
1. Braille, Louis, 1809–1852—Juvenile literature. 2. Blind teachers—France—
Biography—Juvenile literature. 3. Braille—Juvenile literature. [1. Braille, Louis,
1809–1852. 2. Blind. 3. Teachers. 4. Physically handicapped. 5. Braille.]
I. Kiesler, Kate, ill. II. Title.
HV1624.B65F74   1997
686.2'82'092—dc20
[B]   95-52353
CIP
AC

EB 30
4500708409

*To Richard Billett
for the gift of friendship*

ACKNOWLEDGMENTS

The author is grateful to Leslie Rosen, Director of
Information, American Foundation for the Blind,
for helpful suggestions and advice. Many thanks
also to Pierre Cassagne, custodian of the
Louis Braille Birthplace Municipal Museum,
and to the hospitable people of Coupvray.

Contents

The Dormitory

The dormitory was dark and still. Only one boy was still awake. He sat on the edge of his bed at a far corner of the room, holding a writing board and a sheet of thick paper on his lap. Working slowly, deliberately, he punched tiny holes across the page with the sharp point of a stylus. Every so often, he paused and ran his fingers across the raised dots on the opposite side of the paper. Then he continued working with his stylus.

He was interrupted by a husky whisper coming from the next bed. The same hushed conversation took place almost every night—the same questions, the same answers.

"Louis? That you? Still punching dots?"

"Shh! Be quiet, Gabriel. It's late. You'll wake up everyone."

"You'd better quit and get some rest, Louis. The director will be furious if you doze off in class again."

"I know. I know. I'm almost finished now. Go back to sleep!"

Louis Braille placed his paper and stylus on a shelf behind his bed. Extending his arm before him, he walked across the dormitory and stood before an open window. He was a thin, handsome boy with the strong features of his French ancestors. Tangled blond hair fell across his forehead. His eyes, tinged with purple, stared blankly from above prominent cheekbones.

Louis was a student at the Royal Institute for Blind Youth in Paris. For months now, he had been punching combinations of dots into sheets of paper. He was trying to work out a system of reading and writing for all those who cannot see.

As it was, blind people could not hope to read or write. The best method yet devised for them was almost useless. Isolated from much of human knowledge, unable to communicate by the written word, they could never share fully in life. It was a fact that Louis could not accept. More than anything else, he wanted to read.

Yet his experiments with dots hadn't accomplished much. His friends told him that he was wasting his time. Perhaps they were right. Perhaps neither he nor any other blind person could ever take his place in the world of the seeing.

Standing at the window, he listened to the regular breathing of his sleeping classmates. From the street below, he could hear the rumble of wheels and clicking of hooves as carriages rolled past on the cobblestone pavement. A warm breeze swept through the window, carrying memories of spring in his own village.

At home, the fields now would feel moist and soft beneath his bare feet. The hills would be fragrant with the smell of new clover. Local farmers would be bringing their first produce to market in the village square.

Reaching back into his childhood, Louis tried to remember what the village square looked like. But he knew it was useless. He had tried to remember so many times before. He could no longer recall the sight of the square, or the fields, or the hills. He could not remember what his house looked like, nor could he picture the faces of his mother and father. The sounds, the smells, and the sensations of home—these were vivid and clear. But the sights had faded and disappeared. He could remember nothing he had ever seen. He had been blind much too long.

The Accident

As a small child, Louis loved to watch his father, Simon, at work. Simon-René Braille was the saddle and harness maker in the village of Coupvray, about twenty-five miles east of Paris. A big man wearing a shiny leather apron, he sat at his workbench repairing straps and bridles, attaching bright buckles to harnesses, and making fine new saddles that would last a lifetime.

In Louis's eyes, his father's shop was the center of the world. It was filled with the tangy smell of curing leather, stretched in great slabs across wooden ceiling beams. Massive rawhides hung on iron hooks along one wall. Oddly shaped tools were arranged in a neat row above the wooden workbench.

Louis longed to handle his father's wonderful tools. He knew the name of each one, but he had been forbidden to touch anything on the workbench. "*Non, non!*" his father would warn when the boy reached for a tool. "No, no, Louis! These tools are not playthings. You must never touch them!"

But the temptation was too strong. One morning, Simon was outside in the courtyard, chatting with a customer. Louis ran over to the workbench. He climbed up on his father's chair, lifted a knee, and hoisted himself onto the workbench. All the tools were there before him—the fat wooden mallets, the sharply pointed awls, the knives as keen as razors. Imitating his father, he picked out an awl. He held it in his chubby fist and began to jab at a stray piece of leather.

Pretending to measure with one eye, as he had often seen his father do, Louis bent his head close to the leather scrap and stabbed hard with the awl.

But the leather was tough and would not give easily. Solemnly, he bent his head forward a bit more and brought the awl down with all his might. The sharp instrument glanced off the slippery surface of the leather. Louis shrieked.

Simon ran into the shop from the courtyard. Blood was streaming down the boy's face. As the harness maker reached for his son and picked him up, he saw to his horror that the blood was coming from Louis's left eye. Clutching the hysterical child in his arms, Simon ran back into the courtyard, shouting for his wife, Monique.

Louis's mother flung open the door of their stone cottage and rushed toward the boy with outstretched arms. Two neighbor women, Madame Boury and Madame Hurault, came out on their doorsteps, saw what was happening, and hurried over. Louis's mother asked for some white linen and fresh water, so she could clean the area around the injured eye. Simon went to fetch an old woman of the village who was said to possess healing powers. She arrived at the scene with some lily water and began to dab gently at the wound as tears mingled with blood on the child's face.

Louis had punctured his eye. He was put to bed in the garret room that he shared with his older brother and two older sisters. By the time the local doctor could be found, the bleeding had stopped.

The doctor gave Louis a dose of calomel, a laxative, and told his parents to cover the eye with compresses soaked in cold water. The bedroom must be kept shuttered and dark, he said. Beyond that, there was little the doctor could do but shake his head and tell Simon and Monique to pray for their son's recovery.

Louis's eye became red and swollen. His inflamed eyelid turned purple, as if from a blow. As he rubbed his injured eye to ease the irritation, he unwittingly spread the infection with his hands to his other eye. At the time—it was the year 1812—there was no known way to control such an infection.

The child's vision became blurred. He stumbled about, unable to find anything but the location of the window. His world grew dimmer and darker until, at last, he stared with an empty gaze.

Simon and Monique tried everything. They took Louis by horse and carriage to the hospital in Meaux, the nearest big town, where they consulted an oculist. By then, the infection had destroyed the corneas of both eyeballs. There was no hope, his parents were told. Not yet four years old, Louis Braille was completely blind.

When the family returned to Coupvray, Monique led Louis by the hand into their house. Simon walked slowly across the courtyard to his workshop and began to carve a little cane.

The Little Blind Boy

Like any child who loses his sight, Louis faced a daunting task: he had to rediscover the world around him. To begin with, he explored his own home with his hands. He felt his way along the cool stone walls and up the stone stairs to the garret. He learned the shapes of the wooden stools and heavy table that stood in front of the fireplace, of the squat cupboard where dishes were kept, of the worn sink with its stone drainpipe running along the wall. He memorized every nook and corner of the house until he could walk about freely without tripping or banging into things. After that, he was allowed to make cautious excursions into the outside world.

At first, he was guided by his brother or sisters. They helped him tap his way with his cane to some of the places he knew well—so many taps along the courtyard to the door of his father's workshop, so many taps to the well behind the house, so many to the vegetable garden beyond. Little by little, he began to find his own way with his cane. He didn't like to be led around by the hand, and his family encouraged him to do things for himself.

His early walks were hesitant, stumbling affairs, but Louis persisted. Tap-tap-tapping, he found his way to the nearby brook, which he could hear gurgling. Then he ventured to the stone bridge a bit farther on. Later, he tapped his way up Touarte, the steep, stony street that led to the village square with its small church.

Every few months, Simon carved a new cane to keep pace with his son's growth. These canes were the boy's eyes. With them, he gradually mapped out the paths, fields, and hills of Coupvray.

As Louis grew older, the memory of things he

had once seen faded, until he could no longer remember colors or shapes. His fingers told him that a tree is tall, with rough bark and veined leaves. But he could not recall what a tree looked like. He recognized people by the sounds of their voices, but could no longer picture their faces. Spring became associated with the sweet smell of wildflowers blooming on the hillsides, of clover springing up among the wild oats. Rain was the sharp wetness on his face. The long summer days were the feel of the hot sun beating down on his bare head.

The hardest lesson Louis had to learn was that his blindness set him apart from the other children in Coupvray. Now and then, a few youngsters would sit and talk to the little blind boy or try to include him in their games. But they soon became restless. Louis couldn't play tag or marbles or hide-and-seek. He couldn't run wildly down the road with a gang of other boys. Sooner or later, the children would drift away to some new interest, leaving Louis behind to invent his own games and imagine private playmates to populate his dark, solitary world.

Everyone in Coupvray knew the blind son of Simon and Monique Braille, and everyone pitied him. They saw him wandering across the fields or lying in the soft moss by the pond at the edge of town, where the other children played. Often, he sat by himself in the village square, his cane over his knees, listening to the sounds of life around him. People would call out as they passed, "Hello there, Louis! How are you this morning?" And hearing their voices, he would call back, "Good morning to you, Madame Boury! Good morning, Monsieur Sequin!"

The village priest, Father Jacques Palluy, took an interest in the sightless youngster who seemed so bright and curious. Louis was seven years old when the priest offered to teach him a few lessons. Two or three times a week, the boy would tap his way up the hill to Father Palluy's house across from the church. They would sit together in the priest's office or beneath the trees in his garden, as

he read stories from the Bible and told Louis about the wonders of nature.

The boy was so eager to learn, Father Palluy felt that he deserved more advanced lessons. He asked the local schoolmaster, Antoine Becheret, to accept Louis as a pupil. In those days, it was unheard of for a blind child to attend a village school. Becheret had never tried to teach a blind youngster. Would Louis be able to learn? Could he keep up with the other students? Becheret had his doubts, but he agreed to take a chance.

Every morning, a schoolboy in the neighborhood came to fetch Louis at home. Hand in hand, they climbed Tourate Street to the one-room schoolhouse above the village. Louis sat in the front row of wooden benches, listening carefully, trying to remember every word the schoolmaster spoke. Because he concentrated so hard, he could usually recite the lesson he had heard the day before. When the teacher questioned his pupils, Louis would answer promptly, without hesitating, often adding a clever or amusing comment. He lived in darkness, but he seemed to have a sunny disposition.

Monsieur Becheret was delighted with the boy's quick mind. In subjects requiring only a good memory, he outshone his classmates. But most subjects depended on reading and writing, and Louis could not hope to read or write. When the other pupils took out their primers and writing slates, he would sit quietly alone, listening to the scratching of chalk and the rustle of pages being turned. The schoolmaster took great pride in the boy's accomplishments, and overlooked his failings. After all, the poor little one was blind. Any accomplishments at all seemed miraculous.

Louis's mother and father, however, could not overlook his failings. They knew that no matter how bright or adaptable their son might be, he could never take his place in the life of the village. Certainly, he could not become a harness maker like his father and grandfather before him. What sort of trade could he learn? What would become of him when his parents were gone? At the time, most blind people ended up begging on the street for a living. The Brailles prayed that their son would have a better fate.

Father Palluy also worried about the boy's future. He discussed Louis with Monsieur Becheret, the schoolmaster. And when visitors from Paris passed through Coupvray, the priest asked many questions about life in the big city. One morning, he boarded the stagecoach from Meaux and traveled to Paris himself, a dusty, bouncing journey that took four hours. When he returned to Coupvray a few days later, he went immediately to the Braille house.

He had visited a wonderful school, he said, a school where blind children were taught useful skills. They learned to make their own clothing and shoes. They learned to play the piano, the violin, and other musical instruments. Ah, but that was nothing! The greatest miracle was this: the poor sightless ones could learn to read and write by a special method. Father Palluy had seen them do this. He had seen it with his own eyes! The students read from big books. They ran their fingers across the pages and read aloud.

Simon and Monique Braille listened with amazement as the priest spoke. They were practical country folk, and they wanted to know everything about this school before making a decision. It is doubtful if either Simon or Monique had ever spent a single night away from their home, or felt the slightest wish to do so. And yet Louis, like the other students, would have to live at the school. He would come home only during holidays and summer vacations. Would their son be happy there? Would he make friends? Would he learn a useful trade?

Father Palluy, meanwhile, spoke to the most influential person in Coupvray, Marquise Jeanne-Robertine d'Orvilliers, who lived in a big castle overlooking the village. She offered to get in touch with the director of the Paris school, and to recommend Louis. Before long, the director wrote to Louis's parents, telling them that the school board had voted to admit their son as a scholarship student. The Brailles were overjoyed.

On the morning of February 15, 1819, six weeks after Louis's tenth birthday, he was bundled up for the trip to Paris. His mother had packed his belongings in a wooden box and stuffed in a roast and some pastries. Everyone in the family lingered in the village square, saying good-bye. Louis stood there solemnly, a thin, narrow-chested youngster almost lost in his heavy coat and thick scarf. A leather cap with earmuffs was pulled down tightly over his head.

Finally, his two sisters and his brother kissed him on both cheeks. His mother gave him a long hug. Then he climbed gravely into the stagecoach beside his father, waved good-bye, and set off for his new life.

The Royal Institute
for Blind Youth

Every morning at daybreak, a loud gong echoed through the ancient building that housed the Royal Institute for Blind Youth. Soon afterward, a rapid tapping of canes advanced down the stairs and along the hallways to the school's dining room, where the students sat down to quick breakfasts of buttered rolls and steaming coffee mixed with scalded milk.

At the end of the meal, an instructor called for silence. He waited for the talk to die down and made the day's announcements. Then there was a rattling of cups and saucers, the rumble of chairs

being pushed back, and again, the tapping of canes as the students crowded out of the dining room and headed for their classes.

These students were taking part in an experiment that had never been tried before. They wanted to prove that blind youngsters were capable of being taught, that they could master their handicap and lead useful, productive lives.

Founded in 1784, the Royal Institute for Blind Youth was the first school of its kind anywhere in the world. When Louis Braille was admitted in 1819, it was still the only school for blind children in all of France. Most sightless youngsters received no education, no training, of any kind. Because they could not see, people believed that they were mentally retarded. Unless their families were wealthy, they usually led miserable lives as ragged beggars who slept in doorways and survived from day to day by the rattling of their tin cups.

Sixty students lived at the school, all of them boys. Louis, the new boy, was the youngest. He was assigned a narrow iron bed in the dormitory and given a uniform—woolen trousers and a jacket with engraved metal buttons. Then one of the older boys guided him around the building through long corridors, up and down worn stairways, and into drafty rooms.

Far from his parents, among strangers for the first time, he felt lost and lonely. Everything seemed so different. He couldn't even find his way around the school by himself. The old building was damp and chilly. The teachers were strict. Boys who broke the rules were put on a diet of bread and water or placed in solitary confinement.

Gradually, Louis became familiar with his new surroundings. He learned to count the steps from his bed to the dormitory door, from the door to the stairs, from the stairs to the dining room, from the dining room to the courtyard. He made his first friend, a boy named Gabriel Gauthier, who slept in the bed next to his. At night, Gabriel would strike up whispered conversations, asking about Louis's family and village, sharing stories and gossip about the school, trying to cheer up the new boy.

The weeks passed quickly. Soon Louis could move about the school as though he had always lived there. He learned to recognize the voices of his classmates and teachers. And he threw himself eagerly into his studies, anxious to catch up. Now he was too busy to feel homesick.

As a new student, his first lessons were in *embossing*, a system of reading and writing developed by Valentin Haüy, founder of the Royal Institute for Blind Youth. Embossing meant pressing large letters of the alphabet into thick sheets of waxed paper. The raised impressions left on the other side of the paper could be "read" by tracing their outlines with a finger. Embossed letters took the place of ink print.

Louis practiced the alphabet until he could print each letter and recognize its shape with his fingertips. Then he was able to write his first sentence: *My name is Louis Braille.* After that, he was ready to enter the reading class where students ran their fingers slowly across big pages of embossed print, bound in heavy volumes propped up on wooden lecterns in the middle of the classroom.

Embossed books were too big to be carried around or held comfortably on the lap. The letters had to be widely spaced and tall enough to be legible to the touch. A student had to tell the difference between *O* and *Q,* for example, or between *I* and *T*. One page of embossed print contained only a few sentences. The thick sheets of embossing paper could be printed on one side only, and individual pages were pasted back-to-back before being bound. Several volumes were needed to contain the text of one small schoolbook.

As a result, embossed books were not only big, but expensive to print. Not many existed. The school's library had only fourteen embossed books. And once a student left the Institute, it was as though he had never learned to read at all, for in the outside world, embossed books were hard to find.

The worst problem was that embossed letters were difficult to "read." By the time Louis fingered his way to the last word of a sentence, he might not remember the first word. Like others before him, he was disappointed. Blind people, he discovered, not only had to walk slowly and hesitantly, they had to read slowly and hesitantly as well. Embossing was a fine *idea*. But it was more a classroom exercise than a practical means of communication. Even so, it was the best method available at the time.

Instead of relying on a few hard-to-read embossed books, the students learned mainly by listening and remembering. They would sit quietly as the teacher lectured. Then they were asked to repeat parts of the lesson or answer questions about it.

As a rule, older boys were taught by sighted teachers. Once they had mastered a lesson, they in turn taught the same lesson to the younger boys. Some of these blind students stayed on at the Institute after graduation and became full-time instructors.

The school's program was a mixture of academic

subjects, practical crafts, and music. Louis spent several hours a week in the school workshop, learning to knit caps and mittens and to make leather slippers, which were sold in Paris shops to raise money for the Institute. He took courses in history, grammar, arithmetic, and geography. His geography classroom had a large relief map of France. The first time Louis placed his fingers on this map, he could actually feel the outlines of the city of Paris. He could trace the winding course of the river Seine into the countryside and feel the sharp pinnacles of the Alps, the mountains in the south of France.

Every Thursday, the students were led through the streets of Paris to the Botanical Gardens. They walked single file, holding on to a long connecting rope, while a sighted teacher described the scenes around them. Passersby would turn to stare at the long procession of blind boys.

Louis paid close attention to his teachers' descriptions, but his own impressions often seemed more real to him. He would listen for the flags

flapping in the breeze along the Champs-Élysées, for the gay laughter and swish of silk as fashionable ladies strolled by, for the rhythmic crunch of soldiers' boots. He knew when they passed a bakery or a greengrocer, if they were walking down a spacious boulevard or a narrow alley. He was aware of fountains playing and pigeons fluttering overhead, of moist shade and rustling leaves when they walked through a park, of the coolness and echoing footsteps when they entered a church. Sometimes he recognized the strange chugging of one of France's early steamboats making its way along the Seine.

But nothing that Louis experienced during his first months at the school captured his imagination more than his classes in music. Here, blindness was no obstacle. The sightless could compete on equal terms with the seeing. For this reason, music was heavily emphasized at the Institute. Many of the students went on to become professional musicians. In Louis's day, more than fifty graduates were playing as organists in Paris churches.

Louis discovered that he was naturally gifted in music. He learned to play the piano and organ by ear. He would practice for hours, bent intently over the keyboard, swaying with the music, aware of nothing but the notes dancing around him, piercing his darkness.

In this world, there was no stumbling, no hesitation, no groping with his cane. When the music flowed forth from beneath his fingers, he could sail off on voyages across the boundless ocean of life, unhampered by his blindness.

Nightwriting

At the end of the school year, students and teachers gathered to celebrate the annual prize giving. In a festive ceremony, Louis proudly received his first honor: a certificate of merit in knitting and making slippers. During his second year, he won prizes in music and arithmetic. "He walked very fast along the path of progress," a school friend wrote. "He soon went from elementary classes to those more advanced."

When he went home for vacation, his family was astounded at how much he had learned. He visited his old school teacher, Monsieur Becheret, who shook the boy's hand and asked about his studies. At the village church on Sundays, he heard Father Palluy chant the mass. He practiced on the church organ, took long walks in the countryside, and dazzled the local children with stories about his Paris adventures. None of them had ever seen the big city.

Louis was just beginning his third year when Charles Barbier, a retired artillery captain in the French army, visited the Institute. Barbier had invented a secret military code based on dots and dashes punched into strips of cardboard. When the cardboard was turned over, the raised impressions of the dots and dashes could be felt easily with the fingers.

Using this code, commanders in the field could transmit simple orders silently at night, such as "Advance!" or "Withdraw!" No matter how dark it might be, sentries at frontline outposts could read the orders merely by touching the raised impressions of the dots and dashes. Barbier called his invention *nightwriting*.

Eventually, he realized that nightwriting might

be useful to blind people. With that in mind, he expanded his dot-and-dash code so that any sentence could be written. In his system, the words were not spelled out. Instead, each word was broken down into sounds. Each sound was represented by a different combination of dots and dashes. Nightwriting now became known as *sonography,* which means "soundwriting."

Captain Barbier called on Dr. André Pignier, director of the Royal Institute for Blind Youth, and explained the advantages of his system. Pignier was interested, but cautious. Other methods of teaching blind students to read and write had been tried in the past, but none of them had been successful. Even so, Pignier was willing to experiment with sonography in the classroom. The students could decide for themselves if the new system had any value.

That week, Pignier summoned teachers and students to a special meeting. They gathered in a large classroom, waiting anxiously, wondering what the director had in mind. When he finally came in, he described the history of Captain Barbier's invention and explained how sonography worked. Then he passed around some samples—a few strips of cardboard with dots and dashes punched into them.

Louis's face lit up with excitement when he felt the raised dots beneath his fingertips. He could tell at once that dots were much more sensitive to the touch than the raised impressions of embossed letters. He kept running his fingers across the cardboard strips as Dr. Pignier talked. At last, something new had been created!

Students and teachers passed the samples around and tried to read the words. Barbier's system seemed complicated, but everyone agreed that it must be given a try.

Before long, sonography held no secrets for Louis and his friend Gabriel. Using sheets of heavy embossing paper, a board to rest the paper on, and a pointed stylus to punch dots and dashes, the two boys practiced writing sentences and passing them to each other to read. It was like learning a new language.

As they grew familiar with Barbier's system, they recognized that it had serious drawbacks. Since the symbols represented sounds only, there were no provisions for spelling, punctuation, or numbers. Many dots were needed to represent a single word, making reading slow and awkward. And many of the symbols were too big to be read with a single touch of the finger.

Other students became discouraged and soon gave up on sonography. The system was just too hard to use. But Louis persisted. Even as a little boy, he had insisted on finding his own way with a cane. That same stubborn streak of character would not allow him to quit now.

He began to experiment on his own, using different combinations of dots and dashes, hoping to simplify Captain Barbier's system. Soon, Louis told Dr. Pignier about his experiments. Pignier, in turn, informed Barbier, and the captain hastened to the school to meet this student who was tinkering with his invention. He was surprised to find himself face-to-face with a skinny twelve-year-old.

Louis had rehearsed for the meeting, going over and over in his mind what he wanted to tell Captain Barbier. He spoke politely, choosing his words with care. He praised the captain's invention, but he was not afraid to point out its drawbacks.

Barbier was a proud military man. He was used to giving orders, with no questions asked! He had worked long and hard on sonography, hoping that the French government would adopt his system as the official method of teaching blind students to read and write. And here was a mere schoolboy who dared to challenge his invention—and a blind boy who was supposed to benefit from it!

Nevertheless, he listened to what Louis had to say. Yes, he had to admit that sonography could be difficult. Perhaps it could be simplified in certain ways, as Louis suggested. But the captain insisted that his basic idea—dots and dashes representing sounds—must not be changed. Barbier defended his system with such feeling, and in such a commanding voice, Louis felt intimidated and did not know how to answer.

After their meeting, Louis carried on with his experiments quietly. He arranged and rearranged combinations of dots until his head was spinning. Time and again, he found himself repeating old combinations he had tried before without success.

He was almost ready to give up when a special event at the school renewed his courage. A celebration was planned in honor of Valentin Haüy, who had founded the Royal Institute for Blind Youth before Louis was born. Haüy had been away from Paris for many years, trying to organize schools for blind students in other parts of Europe. He had returned discouraged and penniless, but he had not been forgotten at the Institute. He was invited back, and on August 21, 1821, students and teachers gathered to pay tribute to the grand old man.

Preparations for the surprise celebration had gone on secretly for weeks. Everyone, students and teachers alike, had helped decorate the classrooms, the dining hall, and the courtyard. But Haüy never saw the decorations. By now, he was seventy-six years old and his own sight was failing. He had to be guided about the school.

Even so, it was a joyous occasion for him. He visited the students' classes, shared their meals, and met each boy individually. When Louis felt the bony hands of the legendary founder clasp his own, he was overcome with emotion. He wanted to tell Haüy about his experiments, but he said nothing.

That evening, everyone gathered in the courtyard for a banquet and musical program. Students recited poetry. The choir sang a hymn dedicated to Valentin Haüy. When it came time for the founder to speak, the school band played and the students cheered as the aged educator groped his way across the room with the aid of guiding cords.

With a trembling voice, Haüy recalled his struggles and triumphs during a lifetime of service to blind youth. Much had been accomplished, he said, but so much more remained to be done. The students crowded around him after he spoke, and he embraced them in tears, exclaiming, "It is God who has done everything!"

Valentin Haüy never visited the school again. He died a few months later, totally blind. But Louis could not forget his meeting with Haüy or the great man's words. He felt that Haüy, with a touch of his hands, had personally passed along a torch. Louis wanted to take that torch and hold it high, so it would bring light to all who cannot see. He promised himself that he would go on with his experiments.

The Braille Cell

Visions of dots and more dots danced in Louis's head. He wanted to simplify Captain Barbier's system so that each dotted symbol could be "read" with a quick touch of the finger.

His days were filled with classes and school activities, so he experimented whenever he could find the time—between classes, on weekends, at night in the dormitory. When everyone else had gone to bed, and the only sound was the breathing of his sleeping classmates, he would take out his stylus and paper and begin to juggle dots. Often, he would doze off himself, his head nodding, the stylus grasped in his hand as though he wanted to keep on working in his sleep.

On some nights, he lost all track of time. He would be sitting on the edge of his bed, punching dots, when the rumbling of wagons on the cobblestones outside told him that morning had come.

After staying up all night, he fell asleep in class. And like several other students, he developed a hacking cough. Winter coughs were common at the Institute. The old school building always felt damp and cold.

Louis's mother worried about him when he came home for vacation. He looked so pale and gaunt. She wanted to fatten him up, and she insisted that he go to bed early. Monique would climb the stairs to the garret bedroom, tuck Louis in, and kiss him good-night, as though he were still a little boy.

A few weeks of fresh country air did wonders. Louis's cough vanished. He felt revived. On fine mornings, he would walk down the road with his cane, carrying a stylus, writing board, and paper in his knapsack. He would sit on a grassy slope, basking in the sun and working patiently as he punched dots into paper. People would pass by and call out, "Hello there, Louis! Still making pin-pricks?" They weren't sure what he was trying to do, but whatever it was, he was obviously lost in thought.

Gradually, Louis managed to simplify Captain Barbier's system, but he wasn't satisfied. The dot-ted symbols he came up with were never simple enough. Sometimes he shouted in frustration and ripped the paper he was working on to shreds.

Then an idea came to him—an idea for an entirely different approach. It seemed so obvious! Why hadn't he thought of it before?

Captain Barbier's symbols were based on *sounds*—that was the problem! There were so many sounds in the French language. With sonography, a dozen dots or more might be needed to repre-sent one syllable, as many as a hundred dots for a single word.

Instead of sounds, suppose the dot-and-dash symbols represented *letters of the alphabet?* The alphabet would be so much easier to work with.

Of course, Louis could not simply have one dot stand for *a,* two dots for *b,* and so on. That way, a blind reader would have to count twenty-six dots to read the letter *z.* Additional dots would be needed for numbers and punctuation marks.

But now that he had changed his thinking, Louis made real progress. He invented a simple code that allowed him to represent any letter of the alphabet within the space of a fingertip. At the beginning of the fall term in 1824, he was ready to demonstrate his new system. He had been working on it for three years.

First, he asked for a meeting with the school's director, Dr. Pignier. Louis sat in a big armchair opposite Pignier's desk, a writing board and paper on his lap, a stylus in his hand. He asked the director to select a passage from a book, any book he chose. "Read from it slowly and distinctly," Louis said, "as if you were reading to a sighted friend who was going to write down all your words."

Pignier picked a book from the shelf behind

him. He opened it and began to read. Louis bent over his writing board and paper, his hand flying as he punched dots. After a few lines, he told Pignier, "You can read faster."

When Pignier finished reading the passage, Louis ran his finger over the raised dots on the back of the paper, as if to reassure himself. Then, without hesitating, he read every word he had taken down, at about the same speed as the director had read them.

Pignier couldn't believe his ears. He picked out another book, another passage, and asked Louis to repeat the demonstration. Then, rising from his desk with a burst of emotion, the director embraced Louis and praised him.

Soon the entire school was talking about Louis's new language of raised dots. Dr. Pignier called an assembly to introduce the students and teachers to the new system. Louis sat in the middle of a big classroom, working with his stylus as one of the sighted teachers read a poem aloud. The other sighted teachers leaned forward in their seats, watching Louis's

hand move across the paper. The blind instructors and students cocked their heads and listened as the point of the stylus punched out dots.

Then Louis stood up. He cleared his throat and recited the poem, his fingers moving as he spoke, without missing a word or making an error. When he finished, an excited murmur filled the room and everyone crowded around him.

Louis was just fifteen years old when he demonstrated the first workable form of his system. During the next few years, he would continue to improve and add to his system, but he had already devised the basic alphabet that would open the doors of learning to blind people all over the world.

At first, he used dots combined with small dashes. But as his system was put to use, he found that dashes, while sensitive to the touch, were difficult to engrave with the stylus. Eventually, he got rid of the dashes, perfecting an alphabet made up entirely of dots.

Braille's system seems simple at first glance.

That is the true sign of its genius. A simple system is exactly what Louis had spent three years trying to perfect.

To begin with, Louis reduced Barbier's dot clusters to a basic unit small enough to fit within the tip of a finger. This unit, now known as the braille cell, has space for six dots—two across and three down:

1 ● ● 4
2 ● ● 5
3 ● ● 6

Within this cell, Louis worked out different arrangements of dots. Each dot pattern represented a letter of the alphabet. As used today, the first ten characters of the system represent the first ten letters of the alphabet and the ten Arabic numerals:

A	B	C	D	E	F	G	H	I	J
1	2	3	4	5	6	7	8	9	0

Additional letters are formed by adding dots at the bottom of the cells:

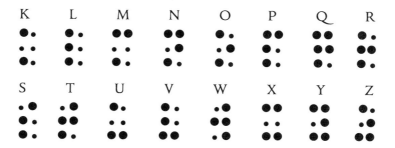

Using this basic six-dot cell, Louis eventually worked out sixty-three characters, representing the entire alphabet, numbers, punctuation symbols, contractions, some commonly used words, and later, musical notation and mathematical signs.

For use in writing his system, he adapted a device Barbier had used to write sonography—a grooved slate to hold the paper, and a sliding ruler to guide the stylus. The ruler was pierced by little windows. By positioning the stylus in these openings, a blind person could punch dots across the page with precision, then slide the ruler down to the next line.

The stylus produces depressions on the paper. One must therefore write from right to left and turn over the paper in order to read it.

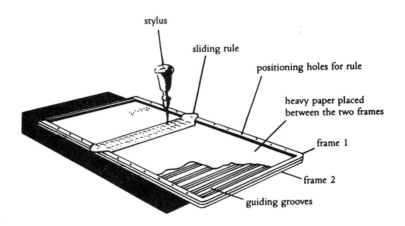

stylus

sliding rule

positioning holes for rule

heavy paper placed between the two frames

frame 1

frame 2

guiding grooves

With this system, Louis swept away all the shortcomings of embossing. The raised-dot characters were simple and complete. They could be read quickly with a light touch of a finger. They took up little more space than conventional printed letters. The braille system, as it came to be known, made it possible to place all the world's literature at the fingertips of blind readers.

The new alphabet of raised dots was mastered quickly by Louis's fellow students. Now, they could take notes in class, write letters and essays, keep journals, record their thoughts and feelings on paper. Louis personally transcribed parts of a standard textbook, *Grammar of Grammars*, into his new alphabet. It became the first text that blind students could read with ease.

Yet he still wasn't satisfied. During his remaining years as a student, he continued to add to his system. Meanwhile, he did not neglect his studies. "Each year," wrote a classmate, "the name of Louis Braille rang out among the winners of the various prizes."

In 1826, while Louis was still a student, both he and his friend Gabriel Gauthier became teaching assistants at the Institute. When Louis graduated in 1828, Dr. Pignier asked him to stay on as a full-time instructor of grammar, geography, and arithmetic. Louis accepted gladly. By now, the school had become a real home to him.

When Louis celebrated his twentieth birthday in 1829, his raised-dot alphabet had been perfected to the point where it was substantially the same as the braille system used today. That year, he published a pamphlet called *Method of Writing Words, Music and Plain Songs by Means of Dots, for Use by the Blind and Arranged by Them*. In his preface, he gave credit to everyone who had helped him develop his system, particularly to Charles Barbier, inventor of nightwriting and sonography. "We must say in his honor," wrote Louis, "that his method gave us the first idea of our own."

The Teacher

Louis had just turned twenty when he became an apprentice teacher at a modest salary of fifteen francs a month. He moved out of the students' dormitory, giving up the bed he had slept in for the past ten years. For the first time in his life, he settled down in a room of his own.

He was able to save enough money to buy his own piano so he could practice whenever he wished. Aside from that, his life changed very little. Apprentice teachers were treated as if they were merely big students. Louis still wore his school uniform, set apart from the students' uniforms by some silk and gold trimmings. And he still had to obey the strict rules of the Institute. He could not leave the school grounds or receive visitors without first getting permission. He wasn't released from those rules until he was promoted to be a regular teacher five years later.

From the beginning, Louis was extremely popular among his students. Being blind himself, he understood their wishes and needs. He knew when to be patient, how to capture the students' interest, how to make them laugh, how to get them to work. "He carried out his duties with so much charm and good sense," one student wrote, "that attending his class was a real pleasure. His pupils wanted to please him. They admired him as a teacher and liked him as a wise and well-informed friend."

The students became experts at using Braille's raised-dot alphabet. By now, Dr. Pignier had authorized the use of the alphabet in all courses at the Institute. Outside the school, however, no one showed much interest. The only method approved by the French government was still the old embossed letter system of Valentin Haüy.

Dr. Pignier tried to convince government officials to adopt Braille's alphabet, but he found that it was not easy to change established customs. Embossing had been in use for nearly fifty years. Braille's new system had not yet been proven, the officials said. The raised-dot alphabet could be used in classrooms as an experiment, but embossing must remain the official method of instruction.

Louis himself wrote to the Ministry of the Interior, the government agency in charge of education. He had no more luck than Dr. Pignier had had. Of course, the ministers had never seen for themselves how well his system worked. Why should blind students be taught an alphabet different from that used by sighted people? they asked. And what about the sighted teachers at the Institute? All of them would have to be retrained. Besides, abandoning the old system would mean throwing out all the embossed books that had been printed at such great expense.

The Minister of the Interior declared that Louis Braille "ought to be encouraged" in his research.

But he was not prepared to adopt Braille's new alphabet.

Louis finally had a chance to demonstrate his system to the public in 1834, when he was twenty-five. The Paris Exposition of Industry was held that year in the Place de la Concorde, a huge open square in the heart of the French capital. Special buildings had been constructed in the square to house the exhibits. Many modern miracles were on display, including the latest steam engine and an electric generator. Dr. Pignier had arranged for Louis to be one of the exhibitors.

He sat at a small table, wearing his school uniform, punching dots as visitors dictated messages or read from books. They were astonished when the young blind professor ran his fingers over the page and read their messages back to them. By now, Louis could write and read his raised-dot alphabet faster than many people could write or read the regular alphabet.

One distinguished visitor was Louis-Philippe, the king of France. He was accompanied by the

Minister of the Interior, the government official who had refused to adopt Braille's alphabet. The king watched Louis's demonstration with polite interest. He asked a few questions and made flattering comments as the Minister of the Interior stood just behind him, smiling and nodding in agreement. Then the two men went on to the next exhibit. Louis never heard from them again.

He became better known for his musical talents than for his invention. Louis was appointed organist at Saint Nicholas-des-Champs, one of the biggest churches in Paris. The magnificent organ at Saint Nicholas became like a personal friend to him, and he looked forward to playing it every Sunday.

At social events he attended with Dr. Pignier, Louis was often asked to play the piano. Complete silence would come over the guests as the handsome young blind man sat down, his hands searching for the keyboard. He would hold his audience spellbound as his fingers danced across the keys, playing everything from Beethoven sonatas to the popular songs of the day.

Louis had mixed feelings about these evenings. He enjoyed going into society and meeting new people. And it was always a thrill when he played well and was rewarded with admiring *bravos* and applause. But he did not want to be regarded with pity, as happened too often, and he hated it when people remarked, "He is so clever for a blind man."

Besides, he tired easily and did not mind going home early. Louis was only in his mid-twenties, but his health seemed to be failing. For months, a heavy sense of fatigue had been creeping up on him. When he climbed the stairs at school, he had to stop and gasp for breath. There were days when he felt feverish and dizzy. The nagging cough that had started during his student days had come back and grown steadily worse.

When he began to cough up blood, Dr. Pignier called in a medical doctor. Everyone knew what the diagnosis was going to be. Louis was suffering from the early stages of tuberculosis, or "consumption" as it was then known, a disease that had afflicted other students and teachers at the Institute.

We know today that tuberculosis flourishes in damp, overcrowded surroundings. But in Louis's day, no one knew what caused the disease. And there was no real cure.

Louis returned to Coupvray for a long vacation. Once again, the bracing country air and plenty of rest helped restore his strength. When he returned to school, he felt fine and was eager to go back to the classroom.

He continued to prepare lessons in his raised-dot alphabet and to transcribe textbooks that were read to him by a sighted friend. He was enjoying his life—his teaching, his music, his many friends at school—when he nearly lost hope that his system would ever win official approval.

In 1840, Dr. Pignier was dismissed as director of the Institute because of his liberal beliefs about education. Pignier had been both a friend and an ally. His dismissal came as a terrible blow to Louis. The new director, Armand Dufau, was a cautious and humorless man. He did not like to take chances. And he did not approve of Louis's alphabet.

Dufau felt that Braille's system was too radical, too different from the conventional alphabet used by sighted people. He said that the raised-dot alphabet would make the world of the blind close in on itself. Once he had established his authority, he banned the use of Braille's alphabet in all classes at the Institute. He insisted on the use of embossing, still the only system to be granted official approval.

Several sighted teachers supported the new director. They feared that they would lose their privileged positions, and maybe their jobs, if the school adopted Braille's alphabet—which could be taught just as well by blind teachers.

To make sure that his orders were followed, Dufau confiscated all textbooks and pamphlets that had been transcribed into the raised-dot alphabet. And he personally went through the dormitory and the classrooms, collecting every slate and stylus he could find and locking them up in a closet.

As a teacher, Louis could not openly defy the

director's wishes. But the students rebelled. They were not willing to give up the only system that made it possible for them to read and write.

Before long, a silent war had broken out between the blind students and Armand Dufau. Quietly, the students collected knitting needles, pencils, nails—anything that could be used to punch dots in paper. They kept diaries in the raised-dot alphabet and passed notes to one another. The older boys began to teach the alphabet to younger ones outside of class. "We had to learn the alphabet in secret," one student wrote, "and when we were caught using it, we were punished."

The Gift

The war over Braille's raised-dot alphabet
finally ended when a young man named Joseph
Guadet came to the Royal Institute for Blind Youth
later in 1840. Hired as Armand Dufau's ·assistant,
Guadet soon discovered that the students were
defying the director's orders and using Braille's
alphabet in secret.

At first, Guadet said nothing to his boss, Dufau.
But he was curious about this strange rebellion
that was going on right under the director's nose.
He had an open mind, and he wanted to find out
why the students were being so stubborn.

Guadet spoke to Louis and to the other blind

teachers. He studied Braille's alphabet for himself. And he met with many of the students. As he watched the students using the alphabet—taking rapid notes, reading with their fingers—he was deeply impressed and totally won over.

Braille's system might be banned from the classroom, but Guadet realized that it could never be banished from the students' minds. After some hesitation, he went to the director and urged him to reconsider. He told Dufau that Braille's system would, sooner or later, be taken up by blind people everywhere. No one, he argued, could stop the adoption of the system any more than he could stop the movements of the sun and moon.

How would it look if the Royal Institute for Blind Youth, the birthplace of Braille's system, rejected that system while the rest of the world embraced it? Here was a chance for Dufau to make a name for himself. Didn't he want to be known as the man who helped launch a system that could change the lives of blind people everywhere?

Dufau listened as his assistant spoke. He

thanked Guadet and promised to consider the matter. At the moment, however, he was busy with ambitious plans to move the school to new quarters.

The ancient building that housed the Institute had long been considered cramped, unsanitary, and unhealthful. A spacious new school, financed by the French government, was completed in 1843. Many changes were to take place when the Institute moved. Students would no longer sleep in a crowded dormitory but would share comfortable rooms. Girls would be admitted for the first time in the school's history. The school's name would be changed from the Royal Institute to the National Institute for Blind Youth.

By the time the move actually took place, Dufau had come around to Guadet's suggestion. He was ready to accept Braille's alphabet and, by so doing, become the benefactor of every blind person in France. Yes, and not only that! He had picked a dramatic moment to present Braille's invention to the public.

That moment came on February 22, 1844, when a large crowd attended the ceremonies dedicating the fine new school buildings. Louis was invited to sit on the stage of the auditorium with the director and distinguished guests. As he took his seat, he could hear the murmur of voices in the audience. His father had died a few years earlier, but his mother and the rest of his family had traveled from Coupvray to be present that day.

Dufau welcomed everyone. The school choir sang, and the band played. Prominent citizens stepped forward one after another to make speeches. Then Joseph Guadet rose to speak.

Guadet had written a little booklet called *Account of the System of Writing in Raised Dots for Use by the Blind*. Published by the National Institute for Blind Youth, this booklet was the first official document to recognize and approve of the braille system. It described the history of the raised-dot alphabet, explained its many advantages, and praised its inventor.

In a voice that rang proudly through the auditorium, Guadet read his booklet to the crowd—to the school's students and teachers, to the assembled friends, relatives, officials, and dignitaries. The reading was followed by a dramatic demonstration. A young girl, one of the new students, was sent out of the auditorium, beyond earshot, while another blind girl wrote down the words of a poem dictated by a volunteer from the audience. Then the first girl returned. With her fingers moving over the raised dots, she recited the poem word for word.

According to school legend, a government official in the audience objected that the demonstration could have been staged. The girl might have memorized the poem beforehand, he argued. She was sent outside again. The official was invited to read anything he wished to the audience, anything at all.

He fished in his pocket, found the stub of an old theater ticket, and read aloud the name of the play, the theater, the date, and the time of the performance, as the second blind girl took down the information with her stylus and slate. Returning once more to the auditorium, the first girl fingered the dots and repeated every word and figure on the ticket as the audience burst into cheers and applause.

Louis was deeply moved by the tribute he received that day, but he scarcely said a word as people pressed around to shake his hand and congratulate him. "Braille was modest, too modest," Joseph Guadet wrote. "Those around him did not appreciate him, or at least were wrong to leave him in the shade. We were perhaps the first to give him his proper place in the eyes of the public . . . in making known the full significance of his invention."

With the school settled in its new quarters, Louis enjoyed periods of improved health. He wasn't as strong as before, however, and he had to speak softly in the classroom, so as not to tire himself or strain his lungs. He knew that his illness could not be cured. The fevers and cough would come and go, but they would always come back. He would

never be completely well again. Meanwhile, he was determined to live as fully as he could.

Two blind friends from his student days, Gabriel Gauthier and Hippolyte Coltat, were now fellow teachers, and he spent much time with them. A young sighted student read them the latest newspapers. They discussed current events, talked endlessly about the people they knew, told stories, exchanged jokes. "Louis would have sacrificed everything for friendship," said Coltat, "his time, his health, and his possessions."

By now, Louis considered his alphabet a completely worked-out invention, which needed only to become widely known. His system was just beginning to spread to schools for the blind in other countries. Different methods of printing the raised-dot alphabet were being tried out. Louis kept in touch with his former students, wrote to them regularly, and sent them books and writing instruments. Often he paid them to copy books in braille, then gave the copies to others. "He never wanted to be thanked," said a friend.

Around 1850, Louis's strength began to fail for the last time. His voice was very weak now, and he could hardly be heard as he lectured. Finally, he had to give up teaching for good. He spent his last months confined to bed, surrounded by loving friends, comforted by the knowledge that his life's work had not been in vain. "I am convinced that my mission on earth is finished," he said.

He died on January 6, 1852, two days after his forty-third birthday. "His friends and his brother gathered around him and embraced him for the last time," wrote Coltat. "To each he gave the most touching tokens of his affection, and when he could no longer speak, he moved his lips. . . . All those present were moved to tears."

After his death, a wooden box found in his room showed how generous he had been. It was marked: "To be burned without opening." Out of curiosity, the box was opened. It was filled with slips of paper, each one a record of a gift or loan made to needy students and friends out of Louis's earnings as a teacher and organist. His wish was respected, and all the paper slips were destroyed.

In his short lifetime, Louis Braille had done more than anyone in history to bring blind people into the mainstream of life. Yet the Paris newspapers did not devote a single line to his passing.

Today, the saddler's son from Coupvray has received the highest honor his country can bestow. He rests in the Pantheon in Paris, the burial place of France's greatest heroes. The braille system is in use throughout the world, in nearly every country and every language. It has been adapted to African dialects and to the complexities of the Chinese ideogram. Networks of braille libraries offer blind people a vast range of reading material from specialized technical works to popular magazines. The slate and stylus today are lightweight, portable tools, while braille typewriters and computer printers keep pace with the latest technology. Other than sight itself, no gift could be more precious to the blind.

Braille's stone house in Coupvray has been pre-

served as a museum and is much the same today as it was when he was growing up there. A plaque on the front of the house reads:

IN THIS HOUSE
ON JANUARY 4, 1809
WAS BORN
LOUIS BRAILLE
THE INVENTOR OF THE SYSTEM OF
WRITING IN RAISED DOTS FOR USE
BY THE BLIND

HE OPENED THE DOORS OF
KNOWLEDGE TO ALL THOSE
WHO CANNOT SEE

The public square in Coupvray, where the boy Louis once sat in the sun with his cane over his knees, is now called Braille Square and is the site of a modest marble monument. On one side of the monument, a relief statue shows Louis teaching a blind child to read. The other side is inscribed with the alphabet of raised dots invented by the fifteen-year-old boy who triumphed over his blindness and helped those like him to do the same.

Index